CHIPS & SALSA!

CHIPS & SALSA!

CHILDREN (YOUTH) IN PLAYS: SHORT AND LIVELY SACRED ACTION

CAROLYN BOHLER

Bridge Resources
Louisville, Kentucky

Unless otherwise noted, Scripture quotations are from the New Revised Standard Version of the Bible, copyright © 1989 by the Division of Christian Education of the National Council of the Churches of Christ in the U.S.A. Used by permission.

Every effort has been made to trace copyrights on the materials included in this book. If any copyrighted material has nevertheless been included without permission and due acknowledgment, proper credit will be inserted in future printings after notice has been received.

Grateful acknowledgment is made to Vince Patton, Associate for Curriculum Development, Youth and Young Adults, and Linda Campisano, Administrative Assistant for Youth and Young Adult Ministries, who appear on the cover and throughout the book.

Edited by Vince Patton

Book and cover design by Robert McAtee

Photography by Robert McAtee

First edition

Published by Bridge Resources
Louisville, Kentucky

Web site address: http://www.bridgeresources.org

PRINTED IN THE UNITED STATES OF AMERICA

98 99 00 01 02 03 04 05 06 07 – 10 9 8 7 6 5 4 3 2 1

Library of Congress Cataloging-in-Publication Data

Bohler, Carolyn Stahl, date.
    Chips & salsa! : Children (youth) in plays : short and lively
sacred action / Carolyn Bohler. – 1st ed.
      p.   cm.
   ISBN 1-57895-064-3
    1. Drama in Christian education. 2. Christian education of
children. I. Title.
  BV1534.4.B62 1998
   246'.72–dc21

98-20731

To the youth of Fort McKinley United Methodist Church in Dayton, Ohio, who helped develop the plays and performed them, and to JoAnn Gilmour, who taught these children and many others.

CONTENTS

About the Plays

Plays are enjoyable for everyone. Production inevitably goes through a chaotic stage, but plays are exciting to work on and fun to perform. The final production creates pleasure for an audience as well. Productions of plays strengthen community, foster creative solutions to problems, and build self-esteem as youth are appreciated for their contributions. In addition, youth have an opportunity to

learn new concepts and wrestle with various issues while working on the play.

The plays in this book share many of the same features. All are based on contemporary biblical scholarship, avoid gender stereotypes, are adaptable for a varying number of actors, require little or no musical ability, and have minimal staging requirements—simple props, costumes, and sound.

Each play is presented in a recipe format with "how-to" instructions. Relax. Even if you have no experience in theater, you can follow the directions and enjoy the results. However, some who produce these plays may be chefs of the art. If so, please use your own creative touches to prepare the "dish" to your taste.

Three of the plays relate entirely to the Bible. In one, the youth learn the books of the New Testament and find out how the books were incorporated into the Christian church's canon. In another, they think about the Psalms as songs or parts of liturgy in their ancient context and reflect on the use of contemporary songs and hymns. In the third, the youth take a long look at the Ten Commandments and grapple to figure out what contemporary behaviors those values would require. The other two plays involve two contemporary faith issues: how church involvement relates to caring for the earth and how Christians pray together although persons have different ways of understanding God.

The plays were originally written for youth (junior high and senior high) or older elementary children (fourth- to sixth-graders) of Fort McKinley United Methodist Church in Dayton, Ohio. My husband John has been the church school teacher for the senior-high class for several years, and I taught the fourth- to sixth-grade class for five years.

John and I wrote *The Environmental Quiz Show* jointly. Plans were under way for the youth to lead worship for the Easter sunrise service, and the youth wanted to do something different. Youth are interested in caring for the earth—and they like quiz shows, which are also easy to enact—so this was a guaranteed attention-getting play.

Our older elementary youth produced *The Books of the New Testament Come Alive!* as a closing event for the church school year. Spending several weeks of creative energy on something other than the regular curriculum was just what the youth needed. Younger brothers and sisters of the original cast performed the play again several years later. The main goal of the play is to enable the students to memorize the books of the New Testament, which can be achieved by learning the New Testament Song on p. 37.

The Bible's Top 150 was another spring curriculum supplement. The big red car and the youth's own music made the production the youth's own. By the time this play was developed, I was more familiar with how to include youth in the production process itself. Our son Stephen, then twelve, thought through the logistics of how to include contemporary music in the production and did the mechanical recording. Each church will no doubt have a twelve- to seventeen-year-old who will be interested in and able to do this.

All Praying Alike? was written so that it could be produced by youth at a week-long bike camp. They wanted something to do in the evenings that was enjoyable and that had some devotional quality. Since I did not have the advantage of actually working with those in the play, my daughter Alexandra helped me think through the continuity of the piece and edit it. We wrote the play, made enough copies of the script, gathered the small amount of basic equipment needed, and placed everything in a small box. We called it a "play-in-a-box" for the youth to take on their trip.

Finally, *A Command(ment) Performance* was written because our minister suggested during a children's sermon that the children learn the Ten Commandments. Two months later, our older elementary class presented the skit during another children's sermon in response to the minister's challenge.

How to Perform the Plays

Plays bridge generations. The issues addressed in the plays are of interest to both youth and adults. Adults want youth to know the Ten Commandments and the books of the Bible. Youth want to focus on the environment and music. Both generations have some interest in prayer, and both care about those who are poor, which is a subtheme in the play *All Praying Alike?*

The Environmental Quiz Show and *All Praying Alike?* were written specifically for older youth, but they could be produced for attentive older children. Adults may also be interested in acting out these plays. *A Command(ment) Performance* and *The Books of the New Testament Come Alive!* were written for older children. The simple style of these two plays may appeal less to older youth, unless the plays were offered as skits for a quick study that the youth could perform for each other without much fanfare. The plays can be used as full-scale productions by a youth group or church school class or simply as dramatic readings. I handed out the script for *The Environmental Quiz Show* to seminary students in a course on ministry and environmental issues. I picked a person I was sure would make a good Wizard and gave the individual the script a day in advance. We quickly chose the cast and simply read the play. The actor playing the Wizard, who took the role seriously, appeared in class right on cue when it was time for the character to enter.

The Bible's Top 150 is appropriate for all ages: Adults, youth, and children could work together on the project. Older youth will often "help out" younger children by participating in a children's play, if they are needed to provide enough actors. In our production, we found that older youth were eager to paint the big red car for the younger ones!

A splendid feature of plays is that parents or other family members and friends can and do show up to see the finished product. After church school, parents often ask children and youth, "What did you learn today?" This question is usually answered with something like, "Oh, not much." When a skit or production is visible to all, parents and other adults know the children and youth are learning something, and sometimes youth plays actually inform the adults! For example, several adults who watched *The Books of the New Testament Come Alive!* were interested in knowing more about the Gospel of Mary and the Gospel of Thomas. They had not heard of these discoveries, and they wanted to increase their knowledge.

Preparation

The first four dramas can be performed without the youth studying the issues first. For example, *The Environmental Quiz Show* can be performed without spending any prior time studying environmental issues. Just producing the play itself will introduce facts and ideas that are educational. However, study in conjunction with performing the play could result in a more complete understanding of the topic. The play would be the culmination of the study. If no time is set aside for study preparation, it would be wise for at least the teachers or directors to read the optional study sections themselves, so that they are prepared to insert information while the play is in production.

The shortest of these plays, *A Command(ment) Performance,* requires the use of the study material. The students use the material to make decisions about their contemporary translations, which are then written on the poster boards that serve as their costumes. The preparation for this skit is in many ways more significant than the skit itself.

In some situations, the production of the play may lead to the desire to study the topic after the performance. This optional material is certainly as relevant subsequent to the play as it is before.

Settings

The church I attend is of a medium size, with approximately two hundred members and an average attendance of slightly over one hundred. Approximately two dozen children and youth have been involved in these presentations. Since three of these productions were parts of Sunday morning worship services, we used the sanctuary, which has no special architectural features except a balcony (which is useful in *The Environmental Quiz Show*) and a slightly raised chancel area.

These presentations can all be staged in a sanctuary, on a flat surface in a multipurpose room or gym, or in a more theatrical setting with a stage and curtain. No curtain, however, is needed, since any changes in sets are made in front of the audience. Also, there is no need for any background scenery.

Sound

A few microphones are needed for all but the most intimate settings. These are for the actors who speak consistently throughout the play, such as a narrator, the Wizard or Assistant in *The Environmental Quiz Show*, or the teacher in *The Bible's Top 150.* Actors need to be told to speak loudly whether or not they use a microphone. Getting children and youth to do this is very difficult, but it *is* possible with constant affirmation and reinforcement. Do not place one microphone several feet from three characters in an effort to pick up the sound of all three. Youth are inclined not to speak as loudly as they can, because they think that the microphone will help them be heard. It is excruciating for the audience, especially someone who is hard of hearing, not to be able to grasp what is being said. Be sure that the audience is seated as close as possible to the action. Do everything you can to create good sound.

Laughter is a desired accompaniment to these plays. Notice when the youth laugh as they practice the play and encourage them to speak slowly and articulately at those points so that the audience can also hear well and enjoy a laugh.

The only play in this volume that demands any sound system other than a microphone is *The Bible's Top 150,* which requires either a boom box inside the car or a sound technician to turn on the recorded music. *The Books of the New Testament Come Alive!* needs either a pianist (or other live musician) or taped accompaniment for the final song, unless the participants want to sing a cappella.

Props

These plays require only a few props. *The Bible's Top 150* requires a car made from a huge box, and *The Environmental Quiz Show* calls for a quiz show category board. Both of these props are fun to make and provide an opportunity for nonactors to do something noteworthy. Allow the youth or children to make these props. Please discourage adults from taking these projects over, because they are community-building activities that are fun as well as educational for the youth.

Lighting

Lighting is not mentioned in the stage directions. Our productions did not use any special lighting. You can use a spotlight for several of the performances, such as the vignettes in *All Praying Alike?* if you have such resources.

Costumes

Very few costumes are required. The youth can most often wear their usual clothing. However, if the teachers/directors or the youth themselves want to put energy into making costumes, it is an option. For example, when presenting the plays about the books of the New Testament or the Ten Commandments, youth could wear matching T-shirts, gloves, hats, jeans, and so on. While *All Praying Alike?* appears to require—and could use—many costumes for the brief vignettes, none are essential, since the vignettes can be performed completely in pantomime with ordinary clothes.

Actors and Their Roles

Change the names of the characters to adapt to the number of males and females who are available. Some of the characters are named so that they can be either male or female—such as Alex and Terry, and some of the names can be slightly altered—such as Bob (Bobbie), Samantha (Sam), or Jo (Joey). Both girls and boys deserve to try out for virtually all the parts. Only a few characters must be a specific gender, like David in *The Bible's Top 150*. Even this role, however, could be *played* by a female.

It is also possible to change the names in the play according to the racial-ethnic groups and cultures represented in the class. If the youth are mostly of Korean descent, please use Korean names. If the church's youth are mostly European Americans but many Hispanic Americans are in the community, include some Hispanic names. In addition, even if gender or culture is appropriate, some youth just don't like certain names—or they've always wanted to have a certain name and would love to have it at least for the duration of the play. If so, let them change the characters' names!

In addition to changing character names, please feel free to alter any phrases that are confusing or seem peculiar in the group's context. Also add any comments the group wants to make to enhance interest or local humor.

My experience has been that children and youth realize when they are playing a part that is not working out well. Once a fourth-grader who volunteered for a role with a large speaking part realized it was too great a challenge. She readily agreed to change roles. It is probably better to face that situation early in the process than to create a circumstance in which a child or youth is struggling in the actual performance.

Youth seem to be clear who will play which role. The older elementary children do not control their attendance at church school as much as older youth. They will commit to a certain role, but if their parents will not bring them to church school on a particular Sunday, they won't be there for rehearsal—or perhaps even for the performance. Because roles often need to be flexible, it is good to have a couple of adults who can step in at the last minute to play any part. Sometimes a child who has not attended in prior weeks appears on the day of the performance and is consequently the only one without a role. It is useful to prepare some responsibility for any additional persons. If no characters are available, these children can be stagehands or extras in a scene. Like adult theatrical performances, changes in characters can be announced before the play starts.

Rehearsal

Only small sections of a few of the roles in these plays need to be memorized. A cast may choose to memorize all the lines, but each play includes props that are held or are near the actors, so the script (either whole or cut and attached to cue cards) can be read without being visible to the audience. If you choose not to require memorization, stress the importance of familiarity with the lines. It's amazing, however, how some youth who do not sight-read well can perform quite adeptly when they are given a chance to take the part home to practice, practice, practice. Memorizing and reciting lines is easier for some than reading something for the first time. The actors should practice their roles a number of times. Make sure to include a dress rehearsal, with conditions that are as close as possible to the situation of the actual performance.

What a joy to work with children and youth! Frustrations are certainly possible for leaders and for youth, but the church is a place where children and youth are together for many years, growing older in the same community. Plays are booster shots in the curriculum and in worship.

I encourage you teachers, directors, and youth who read this book to write your own plays. The process of considering study options and becoming involved in the production of plays is stimulating. Find some good contemporary scholarship on topics relevant to the lives of young people and proceed with creativity.

Description (Summary)

Susan, who cares a good deal about the environment, is attending a worship service with her friends, Nancy and Tony. As the play opens, the minister is saying the benediction. Susan is disgruntled because she sees no connection between the worship she just witnessed and the real problems of the world. The Wizard appears and challenges

Susan and five other youth to participate in a quiz show with these topics: recycle, reuse, reduce, reverence, rest, and resurrection. They accept the challenge and begin thinking about the subjects. To their frustration, the Wizard occasionally accepts several answers and doesn't always know the right answer. At one point, the youth are divided about an answer, and Terry consults Ecclesiastes for guidance. Then the Wizard disappears and the youth are left to decide what to do about the quiz show and about their concern for the earth. Susan is ready to leave the church, feeling it is not responsive to environmental concerns, but the youth convince her to stay. The game show Assistant invites the congregation to join in a litany of renewal as the play ends.

Cooking Time (Length of Performance)

Approximately 25 minutes

Serves (Appropriate Setting for Performance)

Worship celebration (the sermon)
Easter sunrise service

Earth Day activities

Any youth presentation

Ingredients (Characters)

Minister, intended to be the minister of the church

Susan, a visitor to the church

Nancy, Susan's friend and a member of the church

Tony, Susan's friend and a member of the church

Wizard

Terry, a church youth

Andy, a church youth

Samantha (or Sam), a church youth

Quiz show Assistant to the Wizard

Organist, intended to be the regular church organist

Ushers

Set crew

(*Note:* The cast of eight, plus the church minister and organist, can be reduced by combining the roles of the Wizard and the game show Assistant, or by combining the parts of Terry and Andy and integrating Samantha's lines into the dialogue of Nancy and Tony. The cast can be expanded by adding a church youth to each of the quiz show teams, making four players on each team. The minister could also be portrayed by a youth. A set crew of five is possible, although fewer can handle the set changes.)

Garnishes (Costumes)

- Church youth wear their normal attire for worship, as does the minister.
- The Wizard can wear simple black clothing, with or without a hat, or a full Wizard costume with a robe and a hat.
- The game show Assistant can choose to dress like his or her image of the character or wear regular youth clothing.

Supplies (Props)

- 3 chairs
- 3 hymnals
- 2 tables, long enough for 3 youth to stand behind, side by side
- Posters with "Team 1" and "Team 2" written on them (attached to the front edges of the tables and flipped onto the tabletop so they are not visible)

- Bell
- Lectern (preferably the church's regular lectern) or a music stand
- Music stand to hold the Wizard's script
- Bible (preferably large) for the lectern
- The church altar, if it is movable, with candles or whatever is usually on the altar; if this isn't feasible, an object that looks like an altar with candles on it
- 3" x 5" cards for script prompting, if lines are not memorized
- Microphones for the assistant (standing) and the Wizard (portable)
- Organ or piano
- Game board, large enough to hold 6 big sheets of paper or poster board, with these topics written on them: Recycle, Reuse, Reduce, Reverence, Rest, and Resurrection. These sheets can be torn or taken off, revealing another sheet below with the same topic written on it. Questions are attached to the backs of the sheets of paper, perhaps on 3" x 5" cards. There are at least three sheets for each topic. The board can lean against a wall or stand freely.
- Copies of the "Litany of Renewal" (p. 24), enough for the congregation

The Dish (The Play)

Sanctuary Setting

This play is designed to take place in the sanctuary. If it is not held in such a setting, the goal is to simulate a sanctuary. A balcony in the rear is helpful. If no balcony is available, the Wizard can simply appear at the rear of the sanctuary.

At the beginning of the play, three chairs face the congregation as if those sitting there were in worship. Hymnals are on each chair. (The altar has been moved out of the way, if it is movable.)

The two long tables are angled behind the chairs, so that three youth, when standing behind the tables, will be visible to the congregation.

When the game board is brought in, it will be placed between the two tables so that there is walking room between the board and the tables. The Wizard will face the congregation in front of the board, moving slightly to the side when the Assistant moves to the board so the congregation can see it. The Wizard can place his or her script on a music stand.

The Assistant steps up to a standing microphone to read her or his segments. A lectern, with a large Bible, is stage left and is near the front of the stage.

When the Assistant calls for rearranging late in the play, the two tables are moved out of the way, and the altar is placed in the middle, with candles on the altar.

Youth can place their scripts on the quiz show tables, memorizing (or using 3" by 5" cards) only those portions that take the characters away from these tables.

At the opening, Nancy, Susan, and Tony are sitting in the chairs facing the congregation.

The organist begins playing the closing hymn, "I Sing the Almighty Power of God" (can be found in most hymnals).

Tony and Nancy look at their bulletins to check the hymn number and turn to the appropriate page. Susan does nothing at first. Tony notices this as the minister, standing behind the pulpit, gestures for the congregation to stand. Tony hands her an open hymnal, points to the correct place on the page, and gets another one for himself. All three stand and join the congregation in singing the closing hymn.

Minister: *(coming forward to give the benediction)* In the name of the Creator, who makes and remakes all that is; the Redeemer, who forgives us as we repent; and the Spirit, which is in the community of Christ, go forth into the world knowing that you are loved and called to love. Amen.

(As the minister walks down the aisle to leave, Nancy and Tony sit down to gather their things. The organist exits during the following conversation.)

Susan: *(still standing)* What was that about?

Nancy: What was what?

Susan: What he *["she," if the minister is female]* just said.

Nancy: That was the benediction. It's how the service always ends.

Susan: *(sits down)* What's the point?

Tony: *Benediction* means "good word." It sends the congregation out into the world with one final message.

Susan: Is it the same every week?

Tony: Uh, I don't know.

Nancy: He isn't always awake then.

Tony: I'm not asleep.

Nancy: Your eyes are closed.

Tony: I'm concentrating.

Nancy: Sometimes you concentrate so hard you snore.

Susan: But what's the point of the whole thing? How does what goes on in here have anything to do with what's happening out there? I mean, it's a mess out there. Just take one topic—pollution. Some days you shouldn't breathe the air. We're destroying our ozone layer. We're ruining our water. Did you know that you can catch a disease just by wading in the *[use the name of a local river]*?

Nancy: I don't think that's quite true.

Susan: Yes, it is. You just don't know.

Nancy: Hold on, Susan. I've had classes about the environment, too.

Susan: But those classes don't tell you half of what is going on.

Tony: Which half don't they tell us?

Susan: Okay, wise guy. Do you know how much solid waste we produce in our cities each day?

Nancy: Five pounds per person.

Susan: *(reluctantly acknowledging it)* Yeah, right. But there's a lot more to know than that. Our environment is collapsing out there, and what happens in here is beside the point.
(Tony and Nancy speak at the same time.)

Tony: No, it isn't.

Nancy: That's not true.

Susan: You'd agree with me if you understood the problem like I do.
(The Wizard stands up in the balcony at the rear of the congregation.)

Wizard: That sounds like a challenge to me!
(All three stare in amazement at him.)

Nancy: Who are you?

Wizard: The Wizard of Wilderness. The Guru of Great Ideas. The Quintessential Questioner. I also run a great quiz show.

Nancy: What?

Wizard: Quiz show. You know, questions and answers. I've been told they're quite popular these days. Wait right there.

(The Wizard exits the balcony.)

Susan: Who is that?

Nancy: I have no idea. Do you, Tony?

Tony: He seems vaguely familiar. I've seen him *["her," if the Wizard is female]* somewhere before, but I can't remember where.

Susan: Has this sort of thing happened before? What's he doing here?

Wizard: *(enters from back of sanctuary)* You've asked enough questions, Susan. Now it's my turn. You claim to know more than Nancy and Tony, so let's find out. You stand over on that side; you two on that side. Every quiz show needs a set, so let's make one of our own.

(Susan goes to one table and Nancy and Tony go to the other as the set is brought onstage. Posters with the words, "Team 1" and "Team 2" are made visible. The microphone for the Assistant and music stand for the Wizard are properly situated. The three chairs and hymnals are taken offstage.)

Wizard: Since my questions are going to be tough, you people will need some help. *(He points at Terry, Andy, and Samantha, who are sitting as members of the church congregation.)* You and you go over there *(pointing at Andy and Terry)*. You go up there *(pointing at Samantha)*.

(The three other contestants join their teams: Susan, Terry, and Andy are Team 1; Nancy, Tony, and Samantha are Team 2. The Wizard takes his or her place at the back of the chancel facing the teams and the congregation.)

Wizard: *(explaining topics and game)* Team 1, you choose a topic. Our Assistant will read the question, and you will have one minute to decide on your team's answer. If you are incorrect, then Team 2 gets a chance, but Team 2, even if Team 1 is correct, you may challenge if you think a different answer is also

Susan: We'll take "Recycle." That's something I already do.

Terry: There's a lot more to recycling than collecting our aluminum cans and newspapers; this may be harder than we realize.

Andy: We can do it.

Assistant: *(pulls off the top sheet of paper and reads the question on the back)* When humans recycle, we are just doing what nature does "naturally." Describe the cycle of one of these nutrients: carbon, nitrogen, or sulfur.

Terry: We're doomed!

Andy: No, we aren't. I remember this from helping my brother study for the sixth-grade science test. I know it! *(stands up formally, clearing throat as if reciting)* The nitrogen cycle: Nitrogen blows around in the air, then lands on the soil. The roots of plants eat that nitrogen. Animals eat the plants. Then the animals get rid of the nitrogen, and it goes back into the air.

Wizard: You are correct.

Terry: I'm impressed, Andy.

Susan: Good job.

Wizard: Team 2, what topic do you choose?

Tony: *(looking at teammates)* "Reduce"?

Nancy: Okay.

Assistant: *(pulls off sheet, then reads question)* Most people agree we need to reduce pollution. Which is smarter: to prevent pollution or to clean it up?

Nancy: *(to teammates)* In the long run, maybe prevention is best, but right now, don't we have to clean up what we've got?

Samantha: But the question is, "Which is smarter?" Of course, now we need to do both, but prevention is best.

Tony: "Prevention."

Wizard: Correct.

(A bell rings.)

Wizard: That bell means you get a bonus question: What percentage of environmental spending in the United States goes to prevent pollution? 1 percent, 10 percent, or 20 percent?

Tony: 10 percent sounds good *(not waiting for his partners)*. We say 10 percent.

Susan: Challenge. I know! I know! Only 1 percent of our money goes into prevention—99 percent goes into cleanup.

Wizard: Team 1 gets the bonus point.

Tony: 1 percent? 1 percent? Are you sure?

Wizard: I'm the Wizard. I'm sure. Pick your next category, Team 1.

Susan: Let's go with "Reuse," which should be practical enough.

(Terry nods yes.)

Assistant: *(pulling off the "Reuse" sheet to read the question)* What products did people in the U.S.A. reuse again and again in 1964, but barely reuse at all today?

Susan: *(looking a little worried)* This is a history question. Let's see, our parents were children then.

Terry: Some of them could have been babies.

Andy: In diapers.

Susan: That's it. "Diapers!"

Samantha: Challenge! "Bottles"—all sorts of bottles: soda bottles, beer bottles, maybe even milk bottles.

Wizard: Both right! In 1964, 89 percent of all soft drinks were sold in refillable bottles.

Andy: But recycling bottles is new. They did it better decades ago?

Wizard: Your category was "Reuse." Bottles were reused; the same bottle refilled. In 1993, only 7 percent of soft drink bottles were refilled. No wonder you're surprised. Team 2's turn.

Tony: We choose "Reverence."

Wizard: Assistant, please.

Assistant: *(gets sheet of paper with question)* True or false: Global warming isn't so bad because we can just wear fewer clothes.

Nancy: That's kind of logical. Do you think it's true?

Samantha: I don't know. It sounds too simple.

Nancy: Tony?

Tony: Let's go with "True."

Wizard: Incorrect. Team 1, what is your answer?

Susan: Get real. It's "False." As much global warming as we're headed for in just a decade or two could mean much more than wearing T-shirts instead of sweatshirts. *(She speaks with determination and an unwillingness to be interrupted.)* Warming the average temperature on earth would melt a lot of ice, which would raise the sea level and flood coastal areas. There would be a lot more wildfires. Weather would come in more extremes, like we are already seeing.

Wizard: You're right. A point for Team 1.

Tony: How was that a "Reverence" question?

Terry: When we revere what is on earth, we take better care of it. Wanting to preserve the earth for future generations is about as reverent as you can get.

Wizard: Next category.

Andy: We choose "Rest"—that sounds easy.

Assistant: *(pulling off sheet to read question)* True or false: Farmland needs to be rested periodically from growing crops, but grazing land can be used year after year.

Terry: Farming? Grazing? I just eat the stuff. I don't know anything about growing it.

Andy: Seems like if animals kept eating the grass year after year, it would run out.

Susan: And when animals trample the same territory, that keeps the grass from growing back. We say "False."

Wizard: Correct.

Tony: What's the score, anyway?

Wizard: Team 1 has five points; Team 2 has two. Next category, Team 2.

Nancy: We choose "Reverence."

Assistant: *(reveals question)* True or False: We are the planet's most important species, and we have the right to use the rest of nature for our purposes.

Tony: We're made in the image of God. . . . That's pretty important.

Nancy: We have dominion. It says so in Genesis.

Samantha: But does that mean we can do whatever we want?

Nancy: Right. We should think of dominion as being responsible. God made us stewards–caretakers–of what's on the earth.

Samantha: So it's "False."

Wizard: Right you are. A point for Team 2. Back to you Team 1.

Terry: We'll take "Reuse."

Assistant: *(gets question)* In an ecosystem, do producers or consumers make their own food from their immediate environment?

Andy: My dad "produces" meals from whatever is in the refrigerator. It must be "Producers."

Wizard: Correct.

Tony: We'll go with "Reduce."

Assistant: *(gets question)* True or False: Population is unimportant when considering the environment.

Samantha: I think population is important, but I'm not sure whether it matters to the environment that much.

Nancy: It's not *that* crowded.

Tony: Population is drastically important to the environment! Twice as many people will use more land, more water. The answer is "True." Population is a number one problem for the environment.

Wizard: Correct.

(A bell rings.)

Wizard: Bonus question: What percent of the world population lives in countries with programs to actually reduce fertility: 90 percent, 50 percent, or 25 percent?

Tony: "Ninety percent." The *rest* of the world knows we have to reduce our populations.

Wizard: Yes. Very good Team 1.

Susan: Let's get back to "Recycle."

Assistant: What did Joseph of Arimathea recycle for Jesus?

Susan: Joseph who?

Terry: Joseph of Arimathea, a friend of Jesus.

Andy: He used his family tomb as a burial place for Jesus. The answer is "his tomb."

Wizard: That's right. Team 2?

Samantha: What about "Resurrection"?

Assistant: *(reveals question)* What was resurrected on the first Easter morning?

Nancy: "Jesus' body."

Tony: Jesus.

Wizard: Correct.

Terry: Challenge! Jesus wasn't all that was resurrected that first Easter. There was also the disciples' hope. Their hope had died with Jesus' crucifixion, but it was resurrected three days later.

Wizard: Correct also.

Susan: Shall we try "Reverence"?

Andy: Okay.

Assistant: *(gets question)* Which statement best describes why people act as they do? **(a)** We are individuals seeking fulfillment. **(b)** Everything is connected to everything else.

Susan: Would you please repeat the question?

Assistant: Which principle has a bigger impact on how we live? **(a)** We are individuals seeking fulfillment. **(b)** Everything is connected to everything else.

Andy: We are individuals.

Terry: But we're connected to each other when we care.

Susan: I feel very unconnected, especially when so many people have their heads buried in the sand. Individuals look out for themselves. That's the way it is. The answer is "**(a)**."

Wizard: Some say that is correct.

Susan: What do you mean, "some say"? Is it correct or not?

Wizard: That's a good question.

Susan: What?!

Nancy: I'll challenge. We say "**(b)**." Everything is connected to everything else.

Wizard: Some say that is correct.

Susan: Which is it? It can't be both. Either we are individuals or we are connected.

Tony: We're connected. No man is an island.

Andy: What's that?

Tony: "No man is an island." I read it somewhere.

Samantha: But the kids I see at school act more like individuals than anything else.

Andy: Yeah. "Look out for number one." I read that somewhere.

Terry: No, no. That's not it. We have to be together. Listen to this *(going to lectern)*. It's in Ecclesiastes, a short book in the Bible with a lot of good stuff in it. It has the lines about a time for this and a time for that. Like a time to plant and a time to harvest, or something like that. Here it is: *(He reads Eccles. 4:9–10, as if from the Bible itself.)* "Two are better than one, because they have a good reward for their toil. For if they fall, one will lift up the other; but woe to one who is alone and falls and does not have another to help." Two are better than one. See?

(Just after Terry gets to the lectern and starts reading, the Wizard exits quietly, unnoticed, returning to the balcony.)

Susan: But how do you know if that's true?

Nancy: It just makes sense.

Terry: There's more. *(He reads v. 11.)* "Again, if two lie together, they keep warm; but how can one keep warm alone?"

Tony: If there's enough global warming, we won't have to worry about it.

Nancy: So don't you see we're connected? We do a lot of things together.

Andy: Hey, what's the score, anyway?

(They look around for the Wizard.)

Samantha: Where'd he go?

Susan: *(upset)* Great. Some quiz show this is. The guy with the answers just leaves.

Nancy: But he didn't have all the answers.

Susan: That's even worse. Why did he start asking us questions if he didn't have the answers?

Tony: But you're the one who started asking questions.

Susan: Maybe so, but I'm obviously not getting any answers here.

(Susan starts down the aisle. The Wizard appears again in the balcony.)

Wizard: Whoa. Hold it right there! What's the matter with you?

Susan: No more of your questions.

Wizard: Just one. Where are you going?

Susan: To do something. To make some kind of a difference.

Wizard: By yourself? It'll get really lonely.

Susan: There isn't anybody else.

(The Wizard quietly exits the balcony.)

Tony: *(joining her)* Sure there is.

Nancy: *(joining them)* That's why we're here. To help each other.

Susan: But you guys don't think like I do.

Nancy: We don't have to think alike to work together.

Susan: *(indicating the others)* What about them?

Andy: We'll help, too.

(They return to the chancel area.)

Susan: What do I have to do?

Terry: Show up. Be here. Then we can go out into the world together.

Susan: What about the Wizard? Where did he go?

Tony: Who knows?

Samantha: We don't need him. We have enough right here.

Susan: How do we begin?

Assistant: We can start by singing a song. But first we need to do a little rearranging. Come on.

(The altar is moved to the center, and the candles are placed on the altar. The candles are lit.)

Assistant: Okay. The song is "Morning Has Broken" *(motions toward the audience).* Everybody please stand if you can.

(Accompaniment is played on the piano. The entire congregation sings.)

Assistant: You see, we should think of it as a new day, a new beginning.

Terry: *(at lectern)* Hey, listen to this. It's from that "a time to" list in Ecclesiastes. It says, "a time to keep, and a time to throw away." That sounds like reusing and recycling. People were thinking about it way back then.

Andy: People have been thinking about the environment for a long time.

Nancy: And they've been doing something about it—sometimes.

Tony: But there's still a lot left to do.

Assistant: Join us in the litany of renewal that the ushers are passing out. Please join in on the parts labeled "All."

(The whole cast, including the set crew, enters. They take turns reading the litany (p. 24), a different reader for each line. Cast spreads out into the aisle, toward the back of the sanctuary, and faces the minister, who addresses the congregation.)

Minister: *(addressing the congregation)* In the name of the Creator, who makes and remakes all that is; the Redeemer, who forgives us as we repent; and the Spirit, which is in the community of Christ, go forth into the world knowing that you are loved and called to love. Amen.

[The cast exits the sanctuary, followed by the minister. Everyone sings the hymn, "God of the Sparrow" [can be found in most hymnals], while the organist plays.

Litany of Renewal

There is a crisis in the earth.

It is one of our own making.

We have dominion.

We are responsible.

Our once crystal-clear air is dirty.

Our once pure waters have been
fouled.

We did the deed; we are the despoilers
of the earth.

**All: We have dominion. We are
responsible.**

We have made progress.

Our rivers are cleaner now than a
decade ago,
but they still show the evidence of
our human activity.

**All: We have dominion. We are
responsible.**

Our air is better, too—

A little better.

We must be watchful.

We can't let down our guard.

We have much left to do.

There is too much.

It is too big.

It is too big for individuals.

One person alone can do little.

**All: Working together we can do
much.**

Did we work together before?
Sometimes—

Not enough.

We haven't done as well as we should.

All: We can change.

We can be instruments of
improvement.

It is a new day.

It can be a new beginning.

All: We can change.

It is time for a rebirth,

Time for a resurrection,

Hope grows in the spring.

Hope grows in community.

**All: Working together we can do
much.**

What do we do now?

Go out into the world.

Go out with commitment.

Go out with hope.

**All: We have dominion. We are
responsible.**

The following is a sample one-page bulletin that can be handed to members of the congregation as they enter. Its purpose is to identify cast members (so include actors' names) and to inform the members of the congregation what to do at the outset.

The Environmental Quiz Show
A Stewardship Play
by Carolyn and John Bohler

Cast

Minister	*[name of actor]*
Susan, visitor to the church	*[name of actor]*
Nancy, Susan's friend and a member of the church	*[name of actor]*
Tony, Susan's friend and a member of the church	*[name of actor]*
Wizard	*[name of actor]*
Terry, a church youth	*[name of actor]*
Andy, a church youth	*[name of actor]*
Samantha, a church youth	*[name of actor]*
Quiz show Assistant to the Wizard	*[name of actor]*
Organist	*[name of actor]*
Ushers	*[name of actors]*

The Place

A church much like *[name your church]*

The Time

The present

Closing Hymn

"God of the Sparrow" *(Please stand as you are able and join in singing.)*

Preparation

Time

Four to six weeks is a good length of time to prepare, working approximately an hour a week. The dress rehearsal, and perhaps a few other rehearsals, need to be scheduled near the time of the performance.

Instructions

1. Read through the script without any commitment to casting. Discuss the personalities of the youth in the play and think through who might like to play each role.

2. Find out how many youth want to act, and adjust the number of characters accordingly. It is possible to expand or contract the cast slightly by shifting some of the dialogue.

3 Decide on the casting, and read the script again.

4. Change names according to the gender and racial-ethnic groups represented in your class.

5. Let the youth build the game board.

6. Change any questions or answers to make the play relevant to recent local, national, or international issues.

7 Decide how many chairs, tables, and microphones are needed and where they should be placed. Also decide where the game board will be placed.

8. Think through the options for how the Wizard will appear. Once that is decided, pay special attention to the action when Terry goes to the lectern and reads from the Bible. It is important that Terry walk far enough away from the action to make the audience focus their attention on Terry only. This will give the Wizard the opportunity to leave unnoticed. It will take several trial runs before you are satisfied with the timing of the Wizard's arrival and disappearance. Do what you can to make the Wizard's exit as quiet as possible.

9. Prepare the Wizard's costume. The Assistant may need special clothes, too.

10. The Wizard needs to memorize the lines said while entering and exiting. The youth need to be familiar with their lines when they are not playing the game show. (These lines are best memorized.) They also need to be familiar with their lines during the quiz show.

11. Have each cast member highlight his or her part in the script, so they recognize their roles quickly.

12. Decide on the parts for the litany of renewal.

13. Include the minister and the organist in the final dress rehearsal.

Optional Study Preparation about the Environment

1. A number of resources are available that can be useful to youth or youth leaders interested in studying environmental issues. In *Living in the Environment: Principles, Connections, and Solutions,* 9th ed. (Belmont, CA: International Thomson Publishing, 1996), G. Tyler Miller, Jr., discusses an array of interrelated environmental issues. These include the following: human population, energy resources, pollution (air and water), sustenance of biodiversity and ecological integrity, environment and society, humans and nature, matter and energy, ecosystems, climate and weather, population changes, geological processes, deforestation, energy efficiency and renewable energy, global warming and ozone loss, food resources, solid and hazardous waste, sustenance of wild species, politics and the environment, economics and the environment, and environmental worldviews and ethics.

2. Ask the youth what they are interested in studying. They may want to take a field trip to a nearby water treatment facility to see how their own water is processed. Or they may want to trace how the lettuce on their lunchtime tacos or sandwiches got to their hometown. It might be interesting to calculate the number of hours the lettuce has been in cold storage and how far away it was when it was originally grown. Maybe they'd like to try to buy produce from local farmers for a week.

3. Local Girl Scout and Boy Scout centers are filled with information on local environmental issues. Check out local groups that work for political change to protect some aspect of nature—wetlands, freedom from pesticides, and so on.

4. Check on denominational resources for studies on environmental issues. Plenty of videos and study materials are available.

5. I recommend two theological resources for adults who are involved or can lead discussions with youth: Howard Snyder, *Earthcurrents: The Struggle for the World's Soul* (Nashville: Abingdon Press, 1995); and Jay B. McDaniel, *Of God and Pelicans: A Theology of Reverence for Living* (Louisville: Westminster/John Knox Press, 1989).

6. Even if the youth spend little or no time actually working on or studying environmental issues while preparing this play, they may want to use devotionals

based on reverence for the earth, such as. Stephen B. Scharper and Hilary Cunningham, *The Green Bible* (Maryknoll, NY: Orbis Books, 1993), and Sara Dunn and Alan Scholefield, eds., *Poetry for the Earth* (New York: Fawcett, 1992).

7. Perhaps all the youth want to do is to plant a tree in honor of all their hard work on the play.

Supplemental Reading

Miller, Jr., G. Tyler. *Living in the Environment: Principles, Connections, and Solutions*, 9th ed. Belmont, CA: International Thomson Publishing, 1996.

Description (Summary)

Brian must memorize the books of the New Testament for church school the next day and falls asleep worrying about not yet knowing them. In his dream, the books of the New Testament come alive and reminisce about how they came to be. The Gospel of Thomas and the Gospel of Mary also enter the dialogue, because they were friends of the New Testament books before the Bible was compiled as it is today. These gospels, who have been hibernating for centuries, leave just before Brian awakes to avoid confusing him. The books sing a song to help Brian with his memorization. Brian awakens humming the tune, ready for Sunday morning.

Cooking Time (Length of Performance)

Approximately 20 minutes

Serves (Appropriate Setting for Performance)

Celebration at the end of the church school year

Closing event for vacation Bible school

Sermon for worship, when youth or children are leading the service

Fund-raiser for a youth group activity

Youth camp

Confirmation event

Ingredients (Characters)

Brian, a church school student
The Gospel of Matthew
The Gospel of Mark
The Gospel of Luke
The Gospel of John
The Acts of the Apostles
The Gospel of Thomas
The Gospel of Mary
Paul's Letters
Other Letters
Revelation
Stagehand (or two)

(*Note:* The cast of twelve can be reduced slightly with some of the actors playing two parts. It can also be expanded by having more than two people play the letters; that is, there could be up to twenty people acting out the letters! If necessary, change "Brian's" name for gender and cultural relevance. The books of the Bible need not be gender specific.)

Garnishes (Costumes)

- Brian wears sleeping attire (a robe over his clothes is sufficient).
- The books wear or hold a large poster board with the name of the book on the front.
- *(Optional)* The books can wear matching white gloves (for instance, gloves used by a bell choir), some special style of hat, or jeans or leggings to look alike. The books can also wear clothes that depict some aspect of the book they represent. For example, the letters could wear a mail deliverer's outfit; the Gospel of Luke could wear a doctor's smock.

Supplies (Props)

- Poster board, cut large enough for actors to wear
- Large markers
- 12 large envelopes
- Glitter and glue
- Confetti

- Pillow for Brian
- Rocking chair or bed
- Cane for the Gospel of Thomas
- Teddy bear or other stuffed toy for Brian (optional)
- String or ribbons to affix the poster board to the Books, if they prefer to "wear" the posters rather than hold them (optional)

The Dish (The Play)

Scene 1: Brian's Bedroom

> *The bedroom is in front of the stage or at the front side edge of the stage.*

Brian: *(enters, carrying a pillow)* I'm supposed to remember the books of the New Testament for church school tomorrow. How will I ever do that? Let's see, there's Matthew and Mark, 1 and 2 Corinthians and Colossians, 1 Peter, 2 Peter, Revelation. That's only eight. There are nineteen more! I'm so sleepy, though, I'll just go to sleep. I'll try to memorize them in the morning.

> *(Brian stretches out on a bed or rocking chair, places a pillow under his head, pulls a blanket over his body, and falls asleep. Stagehand(s) walk(s) across the stage slowly, carrying a poster with the word "Dreams" on it, scattering confetti toward the audience.)*

Scene 2: Dream

> *Matthew, Mark, Luke, and John enter.*

Mark: Brian, we'll help you remember the books of what you call the New Testament.

John: The word *gospel* is a Greek word that means "good news." Paul first used the word *gospel*, but he was talking about the message of Jesus' life, death, and resurrection.

Matthew: John, why are you talking about the word *gospel?* That word is never found in *you*. Mark and I have *gospel* in us, but when we say "gospel," we mean Jesus' life. We don't call our books "gospels."

Luke: We got our name, "Gospels," about C.E. 150. Just imagine, we didn't have our first names for more than a hundred years after Jesus died!

Mark: I bet most people wouldn't wait that long to get their first names; we books are much more patient. I'm glad we're called gospels; we do have a lot of good news in us.

John: Actually, we didn't have to wait that long, because we weren't born till long after Jesus lived.

Mark: Yes, you should know, John. I'm the oldest of us four. I was born about C.E. 70, around forty years after Jesus lived. What is in me are stories and memories of Jesus, collected and told by prophets, teachers, missionaries, and community organizers in the decades after Jesus lived. Somehow I got the name *Mark*, and I rather like it.

Matthew: We're almost twins; well, maybe only ten, twenty, or thirty years apart in age. But after living for two thousand years, the age difference doesn't seem like much.

Mark: You copycat. More people read you, since they can find almost anything that's in me in you, too.

Matthew: I think I include so much of you because the person who put me together liked you so much. It's a compliment, Mark. If the readers like me, they've got to like you.

Luke: I admit, the same was done when I was created. I have a lot of Mark in me, too. My author wrote me and my brother, Acts. Come here, Acts!

(Acts enters.)

Acts: Yes, the two of us are meant to be read together, just like children nowadays read several volumes of the *Chronicles of Narnia* together. Luke and I are sort of fat; together we make up one-fourth of the whole New Testament.

Luke: *(looking at Matthew and Mark with superiority)* We were written because our author didn't think *your* authors got the story right.

John: *(skipping, acting youthful)* I'm unique–not like any of you three. I'm as young as Matt and Luke. I was probably written for a bilingual community. Many people, you know, spoke both Greek and Hebrew. I like to be different, but I still tell good news.

(Mary and Thomas enter, walking arm in arm. Thomas has a cane and looks old.)

Thomas: What about us? We—and many of our friends—were around when you were all born. Remember how people told stories from all of us?

Mary: *(points at Thomas)* Thomas, you are old, born closest to the time when Jesus was living, yet hardly anyone remembers you, or me. I think they're finding out about us now, and I get pretty excited about surprising them with the new—well, old—ideas in us.

Thomas: Yes, Mary, we're like long-lost relatives, welcomed again into an extended family. But when you were born, and for about another hundred years, many people loved to read and talk about you. I remember.

(Matthew and John take Mary and Thomas by the hands, welcoming them.)

Matthew: We're glad you've joined us. We've missed you. Right now we're trying to help Brian, who's sleeping over there, remember all the books of the New Testament. You two are not supposed to be here. He may get all mixed up, and he won't get it right tomorrow in church school.

Mark: By the time we were all more than a hundred or two hundred years old *(looking at the audience as if to tell them a secret)*— books live much much longer than people—the people who inherited us decided that we four would be friends forever. They put us together and called us, along with you, Acts, and a bunch of letters, the New Testament.

Mary: So Thomas and I had to hibernate for centuries, while you guys were read over and over and over by millions of people.

Acts: *(saying urgently)* I think we should put ourselves in order, so Brian will be able to remember us.

Mark: I'm first, I'm first, I'm first! I was written first.

Matthew: No, no, Acts means that we should get into the order in which we appear in the Bible, the order which Brian has to know tomorrow.

(Matthew and Mark shove each other a little. Mark tries to be first, while the four Gospels get into their order.)

Acts: If we're like Brian's Bible, then I get to be beside my brother, Luke. *(waving arm to welcome the letters)* Come on in, letters!

Paul's Letters and Other Letters: *(Enter singing to the tune of the Late Show with David Letterman, "Letters, We Get Letters")*
Letters, we are letters,
We are stacks and stacks of letters.

Paul's Letters: Most of my letters were sent to cities. If Brian can just remember the city names, he'll easily recall the names of my letters.

Acts: I wonder if Brian realizes all of us books were written in different languages—certainly not English.

Thomas: Of course. Some of us were written in Hebrew, some in Aramaic, some in Greek.

Other Letters: We're sure glad we got included in Brian's Bible. Of all the letters people must have written, we were chosen. Most of us aren't very big, *(sentimentally)* but you know how people cherish letters that mean something to them, keeping them forever.

Paul's Letters: Parts of me were written by the famous Paul, but now people are realizing more and more that some of my letters may have just used my name, probably to get more attention.

Other Letters: *(pointing at the different letters' names on the Paul's Letters'* *poster)* Look at you. You contain Romans, 1 Corinthians, 2 Corinthians, Galatians, Ephesians, Philippians, Colossians, 1 Thessalonians, 2 Thessalonians, *(takes a big breath)* and next come three letters I like, since they were written like a pastor—even *[name of your pastor]*—would write: 1 Timothy, 2 Timothy, and Titus. Finally, my favorite letter, Philemon, is about freeing a slave. I'm glad that's at the end of you. Freedom's a fitting tribute to Paul, don't you think?

Paul's Letters: *(inspecting Other Letters' names)* You're not so hard to remember. You've got lots of ones and twos: Hebrews, James, 1 Peter, 2 Peter, 1, 2, and 3 John, and Jude. *(sings to the Beatles' tune "Hey Jude")* Hey Jude.

Acts: I think Brian's about to wake up. We'd better get into order. Sorry, Mary and Thomas, would you go hibernate a little while longer? We do appreciate you, but you didn't make the team a long time ago. We'll see you later.

Mary: *(speaking over her shoulder as she and the Gospel of Thomas exit)* But it was not just us that didn't make the team. Many of our friends didn't make it either, don't you remember? At least seventeen gospels were written. Only four were picked.

Other Letters: Brian can't wake up yet. We don't have Revie. *(shouting, looking offstage)* Revie, where are you? *(exits looking for Revie)*

Paul's Letters: *(exits with Other Letters)*

Revelation: *(enters, acting as if he has just awakened, rubbing eyes)* I'm still dreaming a great dream.

Mark: You make about as much sense as a dream. I've never figured you out.

Matthew: Dreams are useful, Mark. I am fond of dreams, myself. I enjoy being in this one, and I like the dreams that are in me. I agree, Revie is like a dream, and that's useful. He sort of makes us books a nice collection. We have experiences of the good news, records of history, letters people wrote, and a dream-like recording—that's a pretty good library.

Luke: A library for Christians.

John: Yes, yes, although you know Christians still read and enjoy an even larger library—not just the New Testament, but also the Hebrew Bible that Jesus knew and quoted so much.

Acts: The books that Jesus, in fact, called his Bible, because he was a Jew, right?

(All the books get in order.)

Mark: Right, we've got it! *(hurriedly)* Now Brian's about to wake up.

John: I don't think it's enough that we get into order. I think we should sing or dance.

Mark: How about a line dance?

Revelation: A song.

All Others: A song?

Revelation: Sure, a song will help Brian remember us.

(Revelation starts singing the song [see p. 37]. After he or she sings it through once, all books on stage sing it through again, stepping forward when their names are sung. Brian starts humming the tune.)

Scene 3: Brian's Bedroom

The biblical books squat down behind their posters so they are not visible. The Gospel of Mary and the Gospel of Thomas peek in, slightly visible at the side curtains. Brian stretches, yawns, and begins to sing the song.

Brian: I had the weirdest dream. I think I can remember the books of the Bible. They seem like friends now.

(Brian walks offstage singing the song.)

New Testament Song

THE BOOKS OF THE NEW TESTAMENT COME ALIVE!

Preparation

Time

This production can be accomplished with approximately four weeks of preparation and an hour a week. An extra dress rehearsal will probably need to be scheduled.

Instructions

1. Read through the script, with the youth reading parts they tentatively choose. Announce that this is simply a first reading, but encourage students to consider parts they might enjoy.

2. Decide how many actors want parts, and adjust the number of characters. The cast can be expanded by having a number of people play the roles of Paul's Letters or Other Letters. It is also possible for one of the letters to play the role of Revelation, if you need to reduce the cast.

3. Discuss options for casting, and read the script again, providing an opportunity for youth to read the lines for the parts in which they are interested.

4. If necessary, change Brian's name to fit the context—adjusting the gender throughout the text.

5. Decide on the casting, and read through the play at least twice with those characters.

6. Prepare the poster-board costumes. Make sure the names of the books and letters are large enough to be visible, with no distracting ornamentation or drawings. Also be sure that the posters are all situated in the same direction—vertically works best for holding the they with two hands.

7. Decide where cast members will enter the stage, how they will stand, and how they will move.

8. Youth can memorize lines or cut their scripts into small pieces, keeping their own parts (with a few lines before and after for cues), throwing away the rest, and taping their segments to the back side of their poster boards.

9. Find a person who knows, "Hey Jude" and "Letters, We Get Letters," to help the students learn the songs.

10. Practice the song every chance you get. Decide whether you will use accompaniment, sing a cappella, or use an audiocassette.

11. Discuss clothing—whether each will just wear regular clothes (except Brian),

or whether they want to have matching gloves, hats, shirts, or jeans.

Optional Study Preparation about the Books of the New Testament

1. The obvious goal of this play is to help youth memorize the books of the New Testament. If the students know the song, they have the books in mind. Think of some ways that the names of the books in the New Testament can be displayed in the classroom. For example, have each student write the name of a book on a poster board and hang it around the classroom.

2. After reading this play once, take time to discuss what it is about. What are the books talking about when they speak of their ages? Explain that they were written long after they had circulated orally. The written accounts were completed decades after Jesus' death.

3. Discuss what is meant by the canon when referring to books in the Bible. (A *canon* is an authoritative list or collection of books accepted as Scripture. For Roman Catholics, the canon was established at the Council of Trent in 1546. However, that council simply ratified the list of books that had been in use since the fourth century. Although Protestants have never formally determined the canon, assumptions are made about what books are in the Bible.)

4. Look together at a Bible with the Apocrypha. Browse through the various Apocryphal and Deuterocanonical books including Tobit, Judith, the Maccabees, and Susanna. Think about and discuss how it would be to decide exactly what is or what is not *in* the Bible when there are many sacred writings circulating. Explain that the culture at the time of Jesus knew these writings primarily by memorizing the Scriptures and telling them orally.

5. Have the students name—or bring in—books that seem sacred to them. Perhaps there are poems, even CDs, that provide inspiration or that speak to them about God. Can they agree on what is "holy"?

6. Explain that the Gospel of Thomas and the Gospel of Mary were discovered by archaeologists in this century. Three fragments of translations of the Gospel of Mary survived from the time they were written. The Gospel of Thomas was discovered in 1945 in Upper Egypt in a famous archaeological find called the Nag-Hammadi library. Biblical scholars knew these gospels existed, because other books talked about them. But until this century, these gospels had been lost, buried in the earth. Pieces of other gospels have also been found.

7. At the library or bookstore, find *The Complete Gospels* or separate copies of the Gospel of Mary and the Gospel of Thomas and explore these together. Notice the similarities to the familiar four Gospels and what is new in these two.

8. Discuss whether the students or their parents or grandparents keep any letters. If so, what makes those letters special? Think about how special a letter would be if there were very few of them.

9. Think about how we send letters to individuals or groups of people. Perhaps our modern-day "newsletter" is a way our pastor (or one of us) can write to the whole congregation, as Paul did in his day. Consider writing one letter from your group and copying it to mail to everyone in the congregation.

Supplemental Reading

Miller, Robert J., ed. *The Complete Gospels: Annotated Scholars Version.* Santa Rosa, CA: Polebridge Press, 1991.

Description (Summary)

Alex, who enjoys the "Top 40" hits on the radio, enters her church school class to find that they are studying the Book of Psalms. David, a fellow student, is—to everyone else's surprise—eager to study the Psalms. The students browse through the Psalms, noting that many of them refer to David. They understand why David enjoys this book of the Bible. The class makes a connection between the 150 Psalms, the top choices of hymns and prayers of the Israelites, and the musical top hits of today. They look more closely at the 23rd Psalm, noting to their amazement that it is written from the sheep's perspective!

Cooking Time (Length of Performance)

Approximately 15 minutes

Serves (Appropriate Setting for Performance)

Long children's sermon during worship

Sermon on a special Sunday, such as Youth Sunday or Christian Education Sunday

Special event surrounding an evening meal at church, for example

Ecumenical event, with Jewish and Christian youth (since the Book of Psalms is common to both)

Youth camp

Ingredients (Characters)

Alex Hill (girl or boy)

Mr. Hill (or Mrs. Hill)

Stephen Hill (If Alex is a boy, change "Stephen" to "Stephanie" so that the
   siblings are brother and sister.)

Pamela (or Paul)

Brett (or Betty)

Bob (or Bobbie)

Jo (or Joey)

Ms. Cooger, church school teacher (or Mr. Cooger)

David

Voice of Minister (can be a student in the class who does not move into the
   scene for worship)

Voice of Radio Announcer

Additional students in the class (optional)

Additional worshipers singing the hymn (optional)

Auto engineers (builders)

Auto painters

(*Note:* You may want to adjust these names so that the children/youth enjoy the
name of the roles they play. The only necessity is that David remains David and that
the first three are a family.)

Garnishes (Costumes)

• Youth wear what they wear to church.

• Teacher wears adult clothing.

Supplies (Props)

• Large cardboard box—the size in which appliances are packed is perfect. It
   needs to be movable and able to seat three people, with two in the front.
   (Our youth constructed the car so that the Hill family walked holding the car
   around them; we painted our car bright red.)

• Hymnal and Bible for each student

• Lectern or music stand for the teacher

• Microphone for the teacher

- The same or a different microphone for the minister's voice, which is heard without the minister being seen
- Radio (boom box) with prepared audiocassette with the following in sequence:

   A segment of a favorite song of the students

   "Counting down, on the all-time Top 40, number 23 is—" recorded by the Radio Announcer

   The Beatles' song, "I Want to Hold Your Hand"

   A segment of another favorite song of the students

- Chairs lined up in two different areas of the chancel/stage: One set of chairs for the church school class faces the audience and are angled toward the teacher, who is standing at the lectern or music stand looking at both the class and the audience. (These chairs have Bibles on them.) A second set of chairs, in two rows, faces the audience directly. These represent the "congregation" during worship. These chairs have hymnals on them.

The Dish (The Play)
Scene 1: The Hill's Automobile

Alex's family (Alex, Mr. Hill, and Stephen) are driving to church in their car. The radio is playing. Mr. Hill parks the car and turns off the motor; the radio goes off, too. (Either Alex can work the radio, turning it on or off as she speaks, or a sound director can do that from offstage. The advantage of Alex doing it is that the sound actually comes from the car, like a car radio. The disadvantage is that she has to act while attending to the recording.)

Alex: Dad, leave the radio on just a minute. I want to hear the next song.

Mr. Hill: Okay, I'll leave it on, but shut the doors and go on into church school as soon as it's over.

Stephen: You're so easy on Alex; you let her do whatever she wants. *(tickles, wrestles with Alex)* Make sure you're not out here for an hour!

Radio Announcer: Counting down, on the all-time Top 40, number 23 is—"I Want to Hold Your Hand."

Alex listens for a while, then turns off the radio and exits the car, walking into church and the church school class humming, "I Want to Hold Your Hand."

Scene 2: Church School Class (4th–6th grades)

Ms. Cooger: Did you have a good week? *(waits for some responses before continuing)* We're going to study the Book of Psalms today.

David: Yeah! I like to study Psalms!

(The other students look at David in amazement because of his verbal enthusiasm. Pamela puts her hand on his head to see if he has a fever.)

Pamela: You say what?

David: I like to study the Psalms.

(The others, including the teacher, are curious about David's excitement. They wonder what he's up to.)

Ms. Cooger: To what do we owe this amazing enthusiasm, David?

David: Well, look at them.

Ms. Cooger: Let's all turn to the Book of Psalms in our Bibles.

(The students and the teacher open their Bibles to Psalms.)

Brett: It's easy to find Psalms; they're about halfway through the Bible.

(They all find the Psalms, then begin turning pages, looking at the Psalms and commenting on them.)

Alex: Psalm 101, "Of David."

Pamela: Psalm 103, "Of David."

Brett: "A Prayer of David."

Bob: "To the leader, of David, for the memorial offering."

Jo: "To the leader: with stringed instruments."

Pamela: "A Psalm of David, when he was in the Wilderness of Judah."

Bob: "Of David."

Jo: Psalm 23, "A Psalm of David."

Brett: I'm beginning to see why David likes studying the Psalms—a lot of these seem to be written by David!

David: You noticed.

Pamela: Did you write them?

(The others laugh.)

Ms. Cooger: Think about when these were written—maybe three or four thousand years ago.

David: My parents chose my name because they were music majors in college, and they met each other in church. David was important in their faith and was also a musician, so why not?

Ms. Cooger: I had no idea there was such a connection between you, David, and the musician, the ancient Hebrew leader.

Bob: Look at these funny names: the Korahites, a Maskil, Asaph.

Brett: Maybe those were names of groups, like The Spice Girls, The Beatles, The Beach Boys. *[Change these names to groups that are popular with the youth performing in the play.]*

(Everyone laughs.)

Ms. Cooger: That may be funny, but it actually may be right. Some of the Psalms *were* linked to musical groups of ancient Israel.

Alex: I never thought that there were musical groups then, too!

Jo: What is this at the end of lots of the Psalms, "Selah"?

Pamela: Here's another "Selah."

Ms. Cooger: Actually, we don't know for sure. Maybe it was some kind of direction to the choir, telling them to do something, like "shout" or "bow down."

Brett: The Psalms sure have a lot of mystery to them. Why study them today?

Alex: I prefer "Oldies but Goodies," like "I Want to Hold Your Hand."

Ms. Cooger: We just found the mysterious parts right away. The world has changed a lot since ancient days, but I'm not sure their *feelings* were so different than ours.

Jo: I had to memorize the 23rd Psalm in the third grade. I received a bookmark with that psalm on it, because I knew it by heart.

Ms. Cooger: Let's look at Psalm 23.

(All turn in their Bibles to Psalm 23.)

Ms. Cooger: How about reading it together.

All:

The Lord is my shepherd, I shall not want.

He makes me lie down in green pastures;

he leads me beside still waters;

he restores my soul.

He leads me in right paths for his name's sake.

Ms. Cooger: Stop a moment. From what perspective is this being told?

Alex, Pamela: *(together)* Perspective?

Ms. Cooger: Yes. Songs and prayers are usually told from someone's perspective. If you, Pamela, prayed, "God, I know you are guiding me as I play goalie today," then the prayer is from *your* perspective.

David: In kindergarten, our teacher read us *The True Story of the Three Little Pigs*. It's a funny book that tells the story of the three little pigs from the wolf's point of view.

Ms. Cooger: That's exactly it. In fact, David, I once saw a minister preach a sermon dressed up like Goliath, telling the story of Goliath and David from Goliath's perspective.

Pamela: So why did you ask about perspective? "The Lord is my shepherd . . . He makes me lie down in green pastures." Isn't it a boy talking?

Brett: Or a girl.

Ms. Cooger: Well, let's read it again.

All:

The Lord is my shepherd, I shall not want.

He makes me lie down in green pastures;

he leads me beside still waters;

he restores my soul.

He leads me in right paths for his name's sake.

Alex: I don't get it. How do we know who's talking?

Ms. Cooger: Do you want a clue?

(Some say "yes," others "no.")

Ms. Cooger: Well, it's from an animal's point of view.

All students: An animal?

Jo: The sheep! The sheep. I see—I never realized that before. The shepherd is making "me" lie down, because "I" am a sheep!

Ms. Cooger: Read on.

All:

Even though I walk through the darkest valley,

I fear no evil;

for you are with me;

your rod and your staff—

they comfort me.

Brett: Jo's right. The shepherd's staff comforts "me" if "I" am the sheep!

Pamela: If you were a sheep, the shepherd would take care of you.

Bob: A shepherd would help you to take right paths.

Alex: Would walk with you through difficult times.

Jo: I've heard that psalm many times, but never knew it was from the sheep's point of view!

Ms. Cooger: It's almost time for church, but I want to ask you, first, what feelings would you say Psalm 23 expresses?

Jo: Trust.

Alex: Knowing God is near.

Bob: Confidence.

David: Are trust and confidence the only feelings expressed in the psalms?

Ms. Cooger: No, because every emotion you have, the ancient Hebrews had, too.

Pamela: Fear?

Brett: Happiness?

Jo: Sadness?

Ms. Cooger: Yes, every emotion. They prayed and sang about their feelings, just like you do in your "Top 40."

Bob: What about anger?

Ms. Cooger: Even anger.

David: The Psalms aren't that mysterious after all; they are just from odd points of view.

Alex, Brett, Bob, Pamela, Jo: *(together)* Like the sheeps'.

(All laugh.)

Jo: And they were told a long time ago when people were shepherds instead of computer specialists.

Ms. Cooger: Time for church.

(They all close their Bibles and begin to leave.)

Scene 3: A Pew in Church

The students are sitting in two rows, casually, holding their hymnals. (Alex and Bob sit next to each other.) If you wish to lengthen this scene, all (including the audience) can sing a hymn introduced by the voice of the minister. The students in the two rows stand during the hymn, then sit for the reciting of the psalm.

Voice of Minister: Please turn now to the Psalter, to read Psalm 137.

All:

By the rivers of Babylon–
> there we sat down and there we wept
> when we remembered Zion.

On the willows there
> we hung up our harps. . . .

How could we sing the LORD's song
> in a foreign land?

Bob: *(to Alex)* I wonder what perspective this is being told from?

Alex: Yeah. Who is speaking?

Scene 4: Hill's Family Car

Stephen: *(running to get the right front seat)* Shotgun.

Alex: *(running after him)* I called it first.

(They wrestle each other slightly, before Alex sits in the front and turns on the radio.)

Stephen: Did you stay in the car very long or go to church school?

Alex: I just heard "I Want to Hold Your Hand," then went in.

Mr. Hill: Alex, when we read that psalm in worship today, something dawned on me. You enjoy the "Top 40" songs today. Well, the Hebrews had their "Top 150"—the Book of Psalms!

Alex: I wonder what *her* perspective was.

Stephen: What?

Mr. Hill: Whose?

Alex: The guy the Beatles sang about wanted to hold the girl's hand. I wonder whether she wanted to hold hands back.

Stephen: What are you talking about?

Alex: You know, the sheep wrote Psalm 23.

Mr. Hill: Wrote it?

Alex: Well, not exactly. The authors acted as if they were sheep and imagined writing it as sheep. I wonder if she wanted to hold hands with the guy.

Stephen: Imagined they were sheep?

Mr. Hill: Hold hands?

(They drive away.)

Preparation

Time

This play can be produced in four to five weeks, working only one hour a week (during church school), with additional dress rehearsals on or close to the day of the performance. Preparation will take five to six weeks if the first two are spent learning more about the Book of Psalms and Psalm 23.

More involved rehearsals are needed if the children/youth choose to memorize their parts. (It is advisable for the Hill family to memorize the segments of the play that take place in the car at the beginning and end of the play; the rest of the lines can be read from small pieces of paper that are placed in Bibles and hymnals, not visible to the audience. The teacher can read her/his lines from a podium or music stand.)

Instructions

1. Read through the script, with (almost) anyone reading any part. Announce that this is simply a preliminary reading, but first give some thoughts to who might comfortably portray certain characters. (For example, some will make a better David, Alex, and Ms. Cooger than others.)

2. Decide whether there are enough (or too many) students for the roles. Adjust the number of characters for your actors by combining some parts or expanding some parts to have fewer or more students in the class. Also, you can use older teens or adults to be Stephen or Stephanie, Mr. Hill or Mrs. Hill, Ms. Cooger, and the Voice of the Minister.

3. Discuss options for who plays what role and read the script again.

4. Decide on definite casting and read through the play with those actors.

5. Decide whether you will keep the names as printed or change them. Alter them according to cultural/ethnic and gender needs.

6. Help the youth/children design, build, and paint the automobile.

7. Practice the play in the setting where it will be performed, deciding who will stand/sit where and how people will move.

8. Prepare the audiocassette for the radio announcer and music. (The young person who plays Alex can be responsible for preparing the cassette used in the car, taping from her/his own CD or the radio.)

9. Make plans for two microphones if you decide you need them.

10. Discuss costumes.

Optional Study Preparation about the Book of Psalms, Especially Psalm 23

1. Give each youth a copy of the "Psalms, Hymns, Songs Worksheet" on page 54. Have each child/youth place a Bible and a hymnal side by side in front of her/him. Open the Bible to the Book of Psalms.

Using the information provided below, guide them as they fill in the blanks and discuss their answers. (You will need to do a little bit of research to find the answers with regard to your own denomination's hymnal.)

- The Psalms are a collection of poems, songs, and prayers that have been used throughout the ages in a variety of settings.
- The Book of Psalms is the hymnbook of ancient Israel.
- The English name for the book, Psalms, comes from the Greek word *psalmos* (sahl-moz), which is an attempted translation of the Hebrew word *mizmor* (miz-more), which means "a 'song' of faith."
- Hymns, laments, and psalms of many kinds stand side by side in the Book of Psalms, just like our modern hymnals, which combine hymns and prayers because they have similar topics or are used for similar occasions.
- There are 150 psalms; 73 include titles that connect them to David in some way. These may have been composed by David or were dedicated to him or intended for use by the Davidic kings.
- A number of psalms were linked to musicians or musical groups, which were associated with the leading of worship and other religious ceremonies in ancient Israel.
- Just as we refer to hymns or popular songs when we talk to one another, the people of the New Testament times referred to the psalms as they shared their experiences with each other. For example, Mary's prayer in Luke 1:46–55 is based largely on Hannah's prayer in 1 Sam. 2:1–10; Jesus cries out in Matt. 27:46 (or Mark 15:34), quoting from Ps. 22.1; and Jesus quotes in Luke 4:10–11 a passage from Ps. 91:11–12. Jesus and his disciples sang psalms, and Paul quoted passages from Psalms in his letters.
- *Selah* (See-luh) appears seventy-one times in the *Hebrew Psalter*. This could be a direction to the choir or congregation to respond in some way (to bow down and pray or to sing or shout, or some other direction). Early Greek translators thought that *selah* was a direction for an instrumental interlude.

- The music for the Psalms was memorized, but it is lost.
- The Hebrews used the Psalms primarily for worship, but also for various religious and social occasions.

2. Bring in to view any of these:

"Life in the Bible Days: Biblical Concepts for Today" video (see p. 53 for information)

Some items made from wool: sweaters, socks, scarfs

Samples of wool that are not made into a garment

Stuffed toy lambs and sheep

Pictures of ancient as well as contemporary sheep and shepherds

Samples of olives, sheepskins, lamb, a ram's horn, cheese, and bread

3. Write the word *sheep* in the middle of a large poster (or on a chalkboard). Write the word shepherds in the middle of another poster (or chalkboard). First, ask the students to list what they associate with sheep, and write the answers around the word sheep, drawing lines to make "spokes" around the word like a hub. Do the same with shepherds (see examples, p. 55).

4. Read a familiar story that is written from another perspective. For example, *The True Story of the Three Little Pigs* (see p. 53 for information), is written from the wolf's perspective. You can, instead, tell a fairy tale, then have the students take turns telling it from another perspective (for example, *Jack and the Beanstalk* from the giant's perspective). Or read a Bible story such as "David and Goliath," then tell it from a perspective that is usually forgotten (Goliath's).

5. If weather permits, take the class outside on the grass. Ask the students to lie down and listen to the words of Psalm 23 as you read it aloud slowly. Read it again, asking them to imagine themselves as sheep. Discuss how the psalm is written from the sheep's point of view.

6. Have the class gather in groups of two to four. Ask each group to rewrite the 23rd Psalm from another perspective. For example, take the perspective of the shepherd, the green pastures, or the sheepfold (see examples, p. 56).

7. Try putting Psalm 23 to music.

8. Listen to some music the students enjoy. Pay close attention to the lyrics. Now think about from whose perspective the song is being sung. Write/sing it from another perspective.

9. Give each student a copy of the Psalm 23 to memorize. (I encourage the use of the NRSV, since it is an attempt to be faithful to the original version.)

Supplemental Reading

Farmer, Kathleen A. *Journey Through the Bible: Job, Psalms, Proverbs, Ecclesiastes, Song of Solomon*, vol. 6. Nashville: Cokesbury, 1995, p. 30.

Scieszka, John. *The True Story of the Three Little Pigs*. New York: Viking Penguin, 1989.

Williams, Michael. *Life in the Bible Days: Biblical Concepts for Today*, vol. 1. Nashville: Graded Press Video, 1990.

Psalms, Hymns, Songs Worksheet

(Use your Bible and hymnal to complete the first part of this worksheet.)

Book of Psalms

How many Psalms are there?

What are "lyrics"?

Where is the music?

Who are the authors?

How was the book put together?

What were the psalms used for?

Hymnal

How many hymns are there?

What are the "lyrics"?

Where is the music?

Who are the authors?

How was the book put together?

What are the hymns used for?

Where do you hear songs you like today?

What does the "Top 40" refer to?

What are some examples of lyrics you like today?

What are some examples of music you like?

Who are your favorite artists? authors?

How is the "Top 40" put together?

What are your favorite songs used for?

Classroom Example of Associations with Sheep and Shepherds

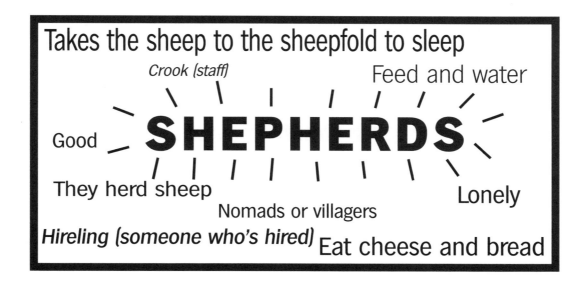

Student Examples of the Psalm 23 from Other Perspectives

From the Perspective of the Sheepfold

I am the hands that hold sheep tight.

I hold them tight lots of cold nights.

Keeping them from harm, holding them in my arms.

Even though they leave every day, I'm still there waiting for the night.

Ready to comfort them when they come to my sight.

From the Perspective of the Green Pastures

I am a green pasture.

Shepherds lead sheep through me.

The shepherds lead them beside the still waters.

The sheep walk through the darkest valley, and the
   shepherd restores their souls.

I notice the shepherd has a rod and staff that
   leads the sheep on the right path.

I comfort and feed the sheep with my grass.

From the Perspective of the Shepherd

I am the good shepherd.

I make them lie down in green pastures.

I lead them beside still waters.

I restore their souls.

I lead them on right paths, for my name's sake.

Even though I lead them through the darkest valley,

They fear no evil, for I am with them.

My rod and my staff, they comfort them.

Description
(Summary)

In a van on their return home from a mission work trip, youth group members reflect on their recent experience with people who were poorer than any they had previously encountered. They decide to pray for those people and others who are poor around the world at their next youth group meeting. Joining hands, each prays a silent prayer. After praying, Lindsay thanks the others for "praying together." What the youth do not know, but the audience does, is the very different ideas of God (and God's power and responsibility in relation to humans) that each of the six young people envisioned in their personal prayers.

Cooking Time (Length of Performance)

Approximately 10 minutes

Serves (Appropriate Setting for Performance)

Children's sermon during worship

Thank-you skit in front of a congregation that supported a mission work trip

Camp setting

Ecumenical event that focuses on prayer

Church school event (ending the year, during Lent, etc.)

World Day of Prayer

Ingredients (Characters)

Speaking Parts

Lindsay

Nathaniel

Emily

Doug

Chad

LaTasha

Nonspeaking Parts

Driver for the van (can be an adult)

Other youth, if more parts are needed

Stagehand (or pixie, or angel, or clown)

Potter God

Grandmother God

Genie God

Jazz Band Leader God

4 jazz band members *(optional;* the Jazz Band Leader God can *pretend* other members of the band are present, or use very large teddy bears or other animals with toy instruments)

Jesus

Disciples *(optional;* Jesus can *pretend* to talk to others or there can be other people in the vignette)

Garnishes (Costumes)

• The youth group members in the van in Scene 1 can wear casual clothing.

• Add some slightly dressier article of clothing quickly for Scene 2.

• Ideas for costumes for vignettes:

Artist's smock for the potter

Grandmotherly clothing

Genie or magician attire

Jazz artist clothing, such as vests

Robe(s) for Jesus (and disciples)

Supplies (Props)

• Chairs or benches lined up to give the sense of riding in a van for scene 1

• Books, book bags, sleeping bags, pillows, and snacks (belongings taken on the van ride)

• Chairs in a circle (or pillows on the floor) for the youth group prayer circle in Scene 2

• Poster board cartoon-like "balloons" for the six vignettes, with appropriate wording (These can be held by the Stagehand, or they can be affixed to a long stick so that the Stagehand moves the stick over the head of those who are thinking, making the balloons more cartoon-like.)

- Pottery items: potter's wheel, clay, some finished pottery items, and/or some pottery in process or pantomime with no props
- Rocking chair, dolls, favorite children's book, stuffed animals (or real animals if you're daring)
- Equipment for either a genie or a magician: lamp or magic wand, scarves, and so on
- Five jazz band instruments: real instruments, toys or cut-out pictures, or pantomime this vignette with no props
- Props to depict Jesus
- Fan to create wind/breath

The Dish (The Play)

Scene 1: Returning from a Mission Work Trip (inside the van)

Lindsay: There are more poor people than I realized. It's not just more people, but poverty is different than I had realized. I hate to admit I felt poor because I had to wear my brother's baseball cleats for softball. Some of *those* people didn't have electricity.

Nathaniel: When Reverend *[fill in name]* prays for the poor, I always thought it was for people in *[fill in with relevant locations]*.

Emily: Well, you know we have poor people—or at least people who are struggling—in our very own church. We say "they," but "they" are sometimes "us."

Doug: Think what it'd be like to have other teenagers come to fix *your* roof.

Chad: Great!

Doug: But kind of odd, don't you think? I mean, I don't like it when someone notices I've got a worn book bag.

Emily: Think what it would be like to know the people in your church were helping you.

Chad: Great!

LaTasha: Yeah, but kind of embarrassing, too.

Emily: It's not that easy to give, but it's not a piece of cake to receive either. My parents talk about their rough times in the past, when they were on food stamps and welfare. Now they try to give a lot.

Nathaniel: I was at your home when they were talking about ways people with money get benefits, but we don't call that "welfare"—just tax breaks or something. We call it welfare or charity when it's poor people who receive.

LaTasha: My neighbors had plenty of money, then they hit hard times—one of them got sick, and the other one lost his job because his company downsized.

Lindsay: Yeah, it's tough for some people.

(The discussion fades out. Some youth pick up a book to read; others lean their heads back on their chairs to fall asleep.)

Scene 2: Church Youth Group Meeting (soon after the work trip)

The same youth are sitting in a circle on chairs or pillows, ready to pray at the end of a youth group meeting. (If you have more people to include in the play, extras can be added here.)

Lindsay: I think we should pray for the people we just met on our work trip.

LaTasha: And neighbors, or anyone having hard times.

Chad: And people who bend over picking crops all day in the hot sun, earning what I do just refereeing one or two games of soccer.

Doug: How should we pray?

Nathaniel: What do you mean, "how?" Just pray.

Lindsay: Okay. Let's join hands this time.

Emily: I agree; somehow praying together means a lot to me right now.

(All join hands and take different postures. Some keep their eyes open. Some bow their heads. The Stagehand—or pixie,

angel, or clown—enters holding a balloon-shaped drawing to indicate a person's thoughts, with the words, "Lindsay's Prayer" on it. The Stagehand goes over to Lindsay, displaying the balloon over Lindsay's head. The youth freeze in their positions while the action moves to the place on the stage where Lindsay's prayer is acted out by the Potter God. The Stagehand moves to that place, then exits.)

Lindsay Vignette

(Potter God is in the midst of forming clay, at a potter's wheel, if possible. Finished and partly finished objects are in the room.)

Lindsay's Voice: God, please make us more helpful to each other. Please make humans care more about each other. We thank you that we were able to go to *[fill in with relevant location]* and help our new friends. Please help them not to be so poor. Please help everyone on earth who has more than they need to share with people who don't have enough. Shape us as you want us to be, caring for each other.

(Potter God exits.)

Chad Vignette

(The Stagehand repeats the actions with the cartoon "balloon," carrying a poster with the words, "Chad's Prayer." The Stagehand walks to Chad, goes to the location of the next vignette, and then exits, while the youth remain motionless.

Grandmother God is in a rocking chair but is clearly healthy and vital. She has an infant wrapped in a blanket in one arm and a child on her lap. She's reading a book to them, while several other children and animals cluster around the chair. It's clear she's caring for many.)

Chad's Voice: God, you've cared for so many people over millions of years. I know you are caring all the time. But we are responsible, too. You try so patiently and hard to teach us to be responsible. I know you can't just force what you want to happen. It's up to us to learn. Yet you love so patiently. I want to feel your love and care, so I can care for others, too. I want people not to feel badly. Thank you for my family who want me to have things I need. But help me also to know what to do in my life so I can share your patient love with others who hurt or need. *(Grandmother God exits.)*

Emily Vignette

(The Stagehand repeats the action with a balloon that says "Emily's Prayer"; moving to Emily, going to the location of the next vignette, and exiting.

Genie God, or god with magic wand, rubs a large magic lamp [or waves a magic wand]. On the lamp or clothing, display a symbol similar to the Nike swoosh [if Nike is still using the slogan, "Just Do It"]).

Emily's Voice: Change the world, God. Give everybody what they need. Why don't you just do it? Perform a miracle. Don't let people starve. Take away diseases. Make more resources on earth, or tell *us* how to make more. You have all the power you need to do what you want. Do it, please.
(Genie God exits.)

LaTasha Vignette

(The Stagehand repeats the action for "LaTasha's Prayer"; moving to LaTasha and to the location of the next vignette and exiting.

Jazz Band Leader God and four jazz instrumentalists, if you are using these, each play different instruments. The leader is also playing an instrument but is clearly in front, very visible, and obviously gesturing when to start and when to end.

LaTasha's Voice: God, guide me to be an instrument of your peace. I know you can't make things happen just because you want to. You are very powerful and persuasive, but you need our help to do things on earth. I am open to your guidance. I want to know how I should help in our unjust world. I am open to learning how to write to lobbyists for laws that are more just for the poor. I am open to knowing where to volunteer to help people nearby. God, I confess I'm not entirely open. I like my life as it is. So, where I am too stingy, please nod to me that I need to change.

(Jazz Band Leader God exits.)

Nathaniel Vignette

(The Stagehand repeats the action with the balloon; moving to Nathaniel, going to the location of the next vignette, and then exiting.

Jesus stands—preaching—or sits—listening and talking with others. Other cast members can be dressed as disciples, or Jesus can talk to an imaginary audience.)

Nathaniel's Voice: Jesus, you cared for the poor when you lived on earth. You told the rich they were farther from heaven than the poor. You cared for the rich, too. You guided them, told them what to do. Are you walking with us now? Help those of us who are poor and those of us who are rich. It's great you're our brother, Jesus. Help us to be the family of God.

(Jesus exits.)

Doug Vignette

(The Stagehand repeats the action with the balloon; stopping at Doug, and then exiting in the direction of the source of wind.

Wind/breath is evident as a fan from offstage blows air during the voice-over.)

Doug's Voice: God, we can't see you, but we know you are blowing upon us, breathing through us *(stops for a time of silence).*

(Wind/breath stops.)

(All God representations quietly return to the stage in the

background. Once they are located, they freeze in a position.)

Lindsay: Let's all say, "Amen."

All: Amen.

LaTasha: I think we'll be guided to know what to do now.

Nathaniel: Jesus is with us.

Emily: God will provide.

Lindsay: God will shape us.

Chad: God cares.

Doug: The spirit certainly moves.

Lindsay: Thank you for praying. When we all pray together, it's got to be helpful. It's amazing how we all pray alike.

All: *(walking offstage)* Yeah.

Preparation

Time

This play can be produced in two to three weeks, working only one hour a week, or in a few days during a camping event. If an impromptu style is acceptable, the play could even be produced with a few hours preparation the same day—or could be presented as a dramatic reading.

Instructions

1. Youth choose temporary roles to read through the script, simply to familiarize themselves with the play.

2. Decide how many actors there will be and whether there are parts for everyone. Additional parts can be created by having more people in the nonspeaking vignettes. Additional youth can also be added to the van or prayer circle.

3. Decide on the roles and read the script again, using the new casting.

4. Decide whether you want to change the names of any of the characters to reflect gender and racial-ethnic diversity.

5 Make a list of things needed for the vignettes, and decide who will gather or make these.

6. Decide where and how the action will occur in the location of the performance. Decide where the various vignettes will be located.

7. Prepare a cassette recording of the prayers, with the appropriate cast voices, or use a portable microphone to pass to the appropriate youth inside the prayer circle. The prayers do not need to be memorized, since they can be read using either method.

8. Practice the vignettes in small groups.

Optional Study Preparation about Prayer and Poverty

1. Discuss each person's experience with financial situations: poverty, having enough, and affluence. Discuss this in relation to youth in other places in the United States and around the world.

2. Use denominational and ecumenical resources about poverty to get up-to-date statistics and to study relevant current issues—locally, nationally, and internationally.

3. Discuss *how* the youth pray. The "Five Little Piggies" nursery rhyme can be used as a mnemonic device to remember five styles of Christian prayer:

This little piggy went to the market. (*Action prayer,* either through rituals or social action)

This little piggy stayed home. (Staying home and imaging; that is, *imagery prayer*)

This little piggy had roast beef. *(Talking to God prayer)*

This little piggy had none. *(Silent prayer)*

This little piggy went wee, wee, wee, all the way home. (*Repeated phrases prayer,* like the Rosary)

4. Look at the characters in the play and notice what kind of prayer they use. All but Doug use the *talking to God prayer.* Doug uses *silent prayer.* Discuss how one could use *imagery prayer* (imagining resources being distributed and shared and imagining people having enough). Create a relevant phrase that could be used as a *repeated phrase prayer* (such as, "Guide us, God, to learn how to share" or "May we use the abundance you give wisely.") Try praying using one of these options.

5. Use resources on metaphors for God—for children or adults. Browse through the Bible to find the many different ways God is named.

6. Look at the chart that shows a variety of metaphors for God and the kind of power suggested by the metaphors (see p. 68). Find the metaphors that the youth in the play use and see whether their prayers match the kind of power that is implied.

7. Using a concordance, look up *prayer* in the Bible. Notice different ways biblical people prayed and the situations in which they prayed.

Supplemental Reading

Bohler, Carolyn. "God as Jazz Band Leader: Divine and Human Power and Responsibility," *Journal of Theology* Vol. CI (Summer 1997): 53–78. Available free of charge from United Theological Seminary, 1810 Harvard Blvd., Dayton, OH 45406-4599.

Bohler, Carolyn. *God Is Like a Mother Hen and Much, Much More.* Louisville, KY: Presbyterian Publishing Corporation, 1996.

Bohler, Carolyn. *Prayer on Wings: A Search for Authentic Prayer.* San Diego, CA: LuraMedia, 1990 (out of print). This book discusses the five styles of prayer: discourse, silence, imagery, action, and repeated phrases.

Cobb, Jr., John B. *Praying for Jennifer.* Nashville: The Upper Room, 1985. It is out of print in its original version, but is available in a play format by James R. Jacobson, *Too Frightened Not to Pray* (Claremont, CA: Process and Faith, 19XX); also Diane Huie Balay, *The Ballad of Jennifer: A*

Chancel Drama (De Soto, Texas, 1997). In this drama, youth question how to pray for Jennifer, who was in an automobile accident. To order, write Diane Huie Balay, 841 Raintree Lane, De Soto, TX 75115. $3.00.

Copeland, Warren R. *And the Poor Get Welfare: The Ethics of Poverty in the United States.* Nashville: Abingdon Press (in cooperation with The Churches' Center for Theology and Public Policy, Washington, D.C.), 1994.

Eisland, Nancy L. *The Disabled God: Toward a Liberation Theology of Disability.* Nashville: Abingdon Press, 1994.

Jones, Major J. *The Color of God: The Concept of God in Afro-American Religious Thought.* Macon, GA: Mercer University Press, 1987.

Saussy, Carroll. *God Images and Self-Esteem: Empowering Women in a Patriarchal Society.* Louisville, KY: Westminster/John Knox Press, 1991.

Suchocki, Marjorie Hewett. *In God's Presence: Theological Reflections on Prayer.* St. Louis, MO: Challis Press, 1996.

Williams, Delores S. *Sisters in the Wilderness: The Challenge of Womanist God-Talk.* Maryknoll, NY: Orbis Books, 1993.

Wren, Brian. *What Language Shall I Borrow? God-Talk in Worship: A Male Response to Feminist Theology.* New York: Crossroad, 1989.

Power Suggested by Different Kinds of Metaphors for God

Metaphor	Kind of Power	Human Responsibility
Potter God	Creative power to try to shape	God needs some human cooperation, but most of the responsibility is God's.
Lindsay: "God will shape us."		
Grandmother God Grandfather God Father, Mother God Friend, Teacher God	Depends on one's idea of grandparents and parents (can be caring, nurturing, patient, wise, comforting, as well as challenging)	While God guides and cares, humans have the responsibility to try to follow that guidance and to seek that comfort.
Chad: "God cares."		
Genie God	All powerful—to make anything happen	No human responsibility exists–God does it.
Emily: "God will provide."		
Jazz Band Leader God Orchestra Conductor God	Very persuasive power—the greatest in the band—but the power depends entirely on the band members to do their part too.	Humans have a responsibility to do their best, individually and with each other, as we all try to understand what God is nodding to us to do.
LaTasha: "We'll be guided to know what to do."		
Jesus Mary Our Lady of Guadalupe	A companion, a fellow worker who understands our problems and is with us as we live	The sense of human responsibility when praying to Jesus or Mary varies from very little—if we expect them to do the work—to a lot—if we think of them as being with us as we act.
Nathaniel: "Jesus is with us."		
Wind, Breath Love, Divine Energy	Empowering presence is available for us if we let this power affect us	Humans are extremely responsible. God blows, breathes, loves, and provides energy, but we must let it in and let it affect us.
Doug: "The Spirit certainly moves."		

Description (Summary)

A minister has challenged some children and youth to learn the Ten Commandments. The youth discover that learning them means much more than memorizing ten rules. In exploring the "backdrop" of the ancient laws, they find  that two Hebrew values influenced all ten laws: purity and property. Understanding the ancient Hebrew world from which these laws arose, the youth take the task of translation seriously. The youth reflect on how the ancient laws apply to their lives today.

Cooking Time (Length of Performance)

Approximately 5 minutes

Serves (Appropriate Setting for Performance)

Designed as a children's sermon, to be performed in worship (could be performed by youth for children or by the children)

Camp setting

Vacation Bible school

Special church school event

Small play during regular church school (especially during the study of Moses)

Ecumenical setting with Christians and Jews

Ingredients (Characters)

Narrator 1

Narrator 2 (*optional:* only one narrator is necessary)

10 people as the commandments

2 Stagehands (to hold up the backdrops)

(*Note:* It is easy to make substitutions at the last minute for absent actors.)

Garnishes (Costumes)

- 10 sheets of poster board for the commandments (Write one commandment on each sheet of poster board; on the other side, a modern-day equivalent.)

Supplies (Props)

- 2 backdrops, each made out of an old flat sheet
- Large markers or paint

Backdrop 1

The first backdrop has these words on it, written near the top, so that the words can be seen over the heads of the commandments:

Backdrop for Moses' Commandments

Purity Laws	**Property Laws**
What keeps you pure as Jews	What belongs to whom

Backdrop 2

The second backdrop has the following words printed near the top:

"1998 *[or year performed]*, United States of America, for young people"

The Dish (The Play)

Setting: The Front of the Sanctuary

Narrator(s) enter and walk to the lectern and pulpit. The commandments enter in order, with the First Commandment in front and line up facing the audience. The First Commandment is on the audience's left. The commandments hold their poster boards so that the ancient laws are visible.

Narrator 1: [Change the wording here to refer to the minister, the youth director, or the church school teacher—whichever makes the most sense in your context. You can also add a greeting, if appropriate.] Reverend [name of minister/director/teacher] asked us to learn the Ten Commandments.

Commandments: We have!

Narrator 2: First, the backdrop. (He/she motions with raised arms.)

Stagehands: (Enter to center stage, each holding opposite ends of both backdrops, the second hidden behind the first. They lift them *up so that the first backdrop is visible to all.)*

Narrator 2: The backdrop is the situation in which Moses understood these laws to be given by God.

Narrator 1: Laws for the ancient Jews were based on two values that were important to them: purity and property.

Narrator 2: Purity laws helped them to be pure, because Jews were often around many people who were not Jewish. Property laws helped them keep track of what belonged to whom.

Narrator 1: The Ten Commandments, of course, were originally told in Hebrew, but we use an English translation.

(One by one, the commandments recite their biblical words loudly and clearly, in order.)

Narrator 2: Notice that First through the Fourth Commandments are about our relationship with God. *(The first four commandments move one step to their right.)* The Fifth through the Tenth Commandments are about relationships between people. *(The last six commandments take one large step toward the audience.)*

Narrator 1: But that's not all. We wanted to know what these commandments could mean for us, young people in the United States, today. These translations assume our backdrop, as they guide us today.

Stagehands: *(let the first backdrop fall to the ground and reveal the second backdrop. Continue to hold up second backdrop high.*

Commandments: *(return to their original locations while turning their sheets of poster board around to reveal the contemporary meanings on the reverse side. They say the modern words loudly and clearly, then they lay their posters down flat in front of themselves on the floor.)*

Narrator 2: Remember, Jesus taught us that it is not enough just to obey laws. We need to think and feel right on the inside. For example, it's not enough *not* to steal; we should *want* the best for another.

Narrator 1: Jews reflected on their laws, trying to understand them in new situations. Jesus was doing just that as he told his disciples that out of all the laws, there are Two Great Commandments:

Commandments: *(Use sign language to sign the two commandments while the narrators speak [see pp. 78–83].)*

Narrators: Love God with all your heart. Love your neighbor (as) yourself. *(The closing can be a song about the theme, an "Amen" by all participants, or the commandments can exit after a bow, followed by the Narrators and the Stagehands.)*

Preparation

Time

This short play can take up to four weeks to prepare, using about a half hour each week. Most of the time can be spent learning about the context of the original commandments and trying to decide what the commandments might mean today.

The production could also be planned in one long session and performed that same day, for example, during vacation Bible school.

Instructions

1. Let the children/youth decide which commandment they will play. Decide who will be the narrators.

2. Give each commandment a sheet of poster board. Ask the children/youth to write the ancient commandment as large as possible on one side, so that it can be seen easily by the congregation. Just write words, so no drawings complicate the ability to read the laws.

3. One by one, determine a contemporary equivalent or paraphrase for each law. There will not be full agreement, and each commandment can elicit enormous discussion. The goal is to be faithful to the whole tradition of Judeo-Christian thought and to help the youth wrestle with making these laws actually apply to them in their current situations. You can explain the term *paraphrase* and be clear that this is what you are looking for.

   • The text surrounding the Second Commandment, regarding idols, can evoke a discussion about God's sense of self and how ideas about God can change over time. God seems to many today beyond jealousy.

   • The Third Commandment can lead to questions about what are bad swear words and "okay words." The main point is using God's name wrongly.

   • There are different viewpoints about how to keep the sabbath holy. Some may interpret that as needing rest or, more strictly, as not doing "work" on the sabbath. One may think of times of rest or devotion on a regular basis for health and wholeness. Some very strict interpretations exist. If you have Orthodox Jews in your neighborhood, point to their walking to the synagogue on Saturday. An explanation of the varying interpretations about which day of the week is the sabbath is also helpful.

- Not committing murder can lead to discussions that range from capital punishment to vegetarianism.
- Today adultery usually means sexual unfaithfulness to a husband or wife. Although some students may discuss the meaning of the word for adults, they may choose to make the contemporary translation relate to them, focusing on faithfulness in friendships.
- Bearing false witness could relate more strictly to legal issues, but it can also be understood as lying.
- The most difficult commandment for many people to understand and find a contemporary meaning for is the last, to "not covet." *Covet* means to desire, fancy, crave, or pine for something or someone. Some people believe that their desire for a shirt that is similar to the one a friend has is simply a desire to have a shirt like their friend, not to have their friend's shirt. Some wonder about role models. There are people we want to be like in some way, but is that coveting?

  Youth groups may want to focus on the differences between the following:
  - wanting what a person has (either a quality or a possession)
  - wanting the other *not* to have it
  - simply admiring what the other has, which may lead to getting (or becoming) something similar for oneself.

  While the whole class is discussing each commandment, the final decision for the contemporary equivalent needs to be left to the person portraying that commandment.

4. Write the contemporary equivalent or paraphrase on the reverse side of each sheet of poster board.
- Some of the paraphrases that class members may choose include the following examples: "Don't take other people's stuff"; "Don't lie"; "Be faithful in friendships"; and for coveting, "Do not have resentful envy."

5. Ask the narrators or some of the students who may be done more quickly than others to prepare the two backdrop props as indicated. (The floor may be the only place that you will be able to write on the sheets.)

6. Practice the play in the sanctuary (or where it will be performed): walking in and standing, speaking, stepping forward, turning posters to the reverse sides, bowing, and exiting.

7. Learn the sign language for the two great commandments (see pp. 78–83).

Optional Study Preparation about the Ten Commandments

1. It is helpful for the teacher/director to read the three versions of the events at Mt. Sinai found in the Hebrew Scriptures: Exodus 20, Exodus 34 (this explanation will probably be quite unfamiliar), and Deuteronomy 5. The events at Mt. Sinai probably occurred between 1400 and 1250 B.C.E. However, the first located record of the code of Moses was written 300 years after the events. The version found in Deuteronomy was written 500 years after the experiences on Mt. Sinai.

2. While these codes have been named the "Ten Commandments," various religious traditions do not agree on how many commandments there are. There are only nine separate injunctions. ("You shall have no other gods . . ." and "You shall not make for yourself an idol . . ." are parts of the same commandment.)

3. Make a chart in the classroom and give each student a list of the ancient Ten Commandments (as found in Deut. 5:1–21 or Exodus 20.) The following is based on the NRSV translation of Ex. 20:1–17.

I am the LORD your God . . . you shall have no other gods before me.

You shall not make for yourself an idol . . .

You shall not make wrongful use of the name of the LORD your God . . .

Remember the sabbath day, and keep it holy.

Honor your father and your mother . . .

You shall not murder.

You shall not commit adultery.

You shall not steal.

You shall not bear false witness against your neighbor.

You shall not covet . . .

4. Given as much time as you have, try to provide the context in which Moses received these laws. In a biographical fashion, this can fit into the life of Moses (starting with Exodus 2):

- his birth as a Levite
- his mother placing him in a papyrus basket near the river with hopes that the Pharaoh's daughter would rescue him
- the Pharaoh's daughter's rescue and nurture
- Moses' outrage that an Egyptian was beating a Hebrew

- Moses' escape
- his work as a shepherd
- his marriage to Zipporah and fathering
- his call by God in the burning bush
- Moses answering that call
- his leadership of the people

5. The context can be framed by discussing the history of the Jewish people and the importance of covenant. The book of Deuteronomy is written in the ancient Jewish tradition of reinterpreting laws for current periods of time. A "covenant" had been formed between God and Noah (Genesis 8—9). Deuteronomy describes how Moses and the people he led tried to understand the covenant and the laws for themselves in their time. This is exactly what we, several thousand years later, are doing in our church school classes.

6. Think about what *purity* means today. Brainstorm a variety of things that seem "pure" or "dirty." This can be quite an amusing discussion. That's okay! If the students really begin thinking about what is considered "pure" and "dirty," then they can begin to see how the laws regulated everyday events. In addition, they can see how what is considered "dirty" differs from one family to another, one century to another, and certainly how it differs over several thousand years.

7. Purity often relates to the "boundaries" of bodies and relationships. It was very important that the Jewish people maintain their identity, especially when they were around many people who were not Jewish. Therefore, beliefs and practices that were unique to them were essential to their purity. Being strictly *monotheistic,* having one God and no idols, was crucial. Maintaining the sabbath was crucial for their identity.

8. Ideas about property have changed tremendously. Today people think of themselves as individuals who own certain things. In the ancient days of the Israelites, households had a strict hierarchy. The father "owned" his wife and children, as well as animals. Although today we would think of stealing as wrongful use of someone else's property, we would not immediately think of "adultery" as a property law. But adultery at the time of Moses was viewed as having sexual relations with another man's property. Murder, false witness, and coveting all relate to the property of other people. Honoring parents is a way of maintaining the hierarchy—so, it too relates to property.

9. Read the narrator's comments from the script and look at the Ten Commandments, deciding as a class which laws seem to relate to purity and which seem to relate to property—or which are a combination of both.

(*Note:* Be careful, as a teacher, not to indicate that children or youth should do *anything* their parents say when discussing the commandment to honor parents. Point out that parents are usually wise and want the best for their children. You can also explain that some parents make mistakes and behave inappropriately with children/youth. We can "honor"—appreciate, even love—a parent and tell another trusted adult if something the parent is doing is wrong.)

Supplemental Reading

Countryman, William. *Dirt, Greed, and Sex: Sexual Ethics in the New Testament and Their Implications for Today.* Philadelphia: Fortress Press, 1988.

Spong, John, and Denise Haines. *Beyond Moralism: A Contemporary View of the Ten Commandments.* San Francisco: HarperSanFrancisco, 1986.

love

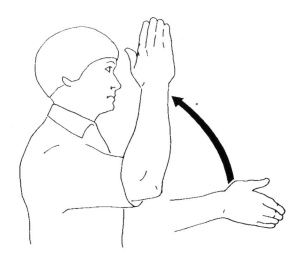

God

with

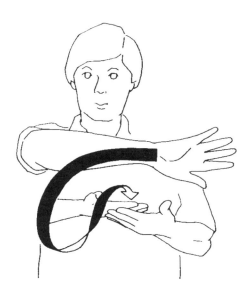

all

your

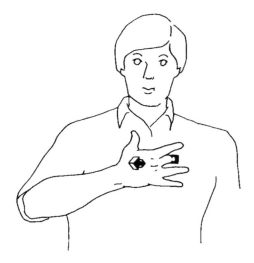

heart

love   **your**

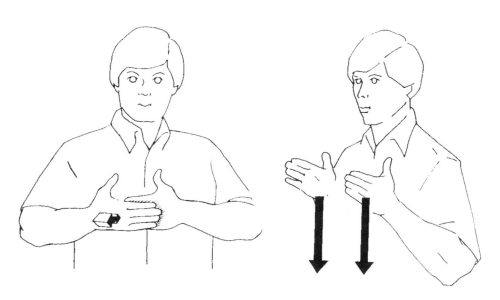

neighbor

yourself

Adapted from *Signs of the Time*, by Edgar H. Shroyer. Copyright © 1982 by Gallaudet University (Washington, D.C.: Clerc Books, Gallaudet University Press, 1982). Used with permission.

Carolyn Bohler is the Emma Sanborn Tousant Professor of Pastoral Theology and Counseling at United Theological Seminary in Dayton, Ohio, and a minister in the United Methodist Church. She has authored several books, including *Opening to God: Guided Imagery Meditation on Scripture, Completely Revised and Expanded* and *God Is Like a Mother Hen and Much, Much More,* a children's book published by the Presbyterian Publishing Corporation.

Her husband John is the director of the Transcultural Program at United Theological Seminary.

Their children, Alexandra and Stephen, are students at Stivers School for the Arts in Dayton. In addition to playing soccer, softball, and baseball, they both enjoy math. Alexandra plays bassoon and studies visual arts; Stephen plays the French horn and studies creative writing.